Nuggets
of
Revelation

Veronica Guard Weekes

TRILOGY CHRISTIAN PUBLISHERS

TUSTIN, CA

Trilogy Christian Publishers
A Wholly Owned Subsidiary of Trinity Broadcasting Network
2442 Michelle Drive
Tustin, CA 92780

Nuggets of Revelation

For information, address Trilogy Christian Publishing

Rights Department, 2442 Michelle Drive, Tustin, Ca 92780.

Trilogy Christian Publishing/ TBN and colophon are trademarks of Trinity Broadcasting Network.

For information about special discounts for bulk purchases, please contact Trilogy Christian Publishing.

Manufactured in the United States of America

Trilogy Disclaimer: The views and content expressed in this book are those of the author and may not necessarily reflect the views and doctrine of Trilogy Christian Publishing or the Trinity Broadcasting Network.

Manufactured in the United States of America

10 9 8 7 6 5 4 3 2 1

Library of Congress Cataloging-in-Publication Data is available.

ISBN: 978-1-68556-204-5

E-ISBN: 978-1-68556-205-2

Dedicated to my children:
Kurt, Dominic, and Asa, the next generation.

Foreword

It is said that it takes up to twenty years for a gold mine to be ready to produce material that can be refined. Significant exploration and development activities must take place to ascertain how to extract and process the gold ore efficiently. Gold processing is a tedious process, and it may take about one tonne of ore to produce twenty grams of gold. Think of it as searching through 50,000 marbles to find one golden marble.

Veronica Guard Weekes has searched deep into the Word of God to find these golden nuggets of truth. This is not an ordinary book; this is a collection of nuggets, and you may take one and hold on to it for a long while before you move to another nugget.

I do hope that the enrichment that comes from reading these golden nuggets of truth will transform your life and move you into a new dimension in your relationship with your Father in heaven. Just as all that was placed in the Holy of Holies was covered in gold, may you be covered with gold as you are ushered into His presence with these truths.

Pastor John Alexander Peters

Preface

In this world of getting, in your getting, get understanding of your purpose for being on this earth, in this world, here and now (Proverbs 4:7 paraphrased).

Acknowledgement

I acknowledge the Holy Spirit, who has never left me alone and who has guided me step by step in writing these nuggets, revealed to me by Him and Him alone.

I acknowledge my dear sisters, by blood and by faith, Linda Guard Tobias and Geraldine Isidore, who encouraged the production and publication of this work. Also, my daughter Asa, who never tired in saying, "I believe in you, Mom. Go for it!"

Introduction

Nuggets of Revelation is a collection of deep truths explained by the Holy Spirit during times of meditation and quiet time with the Lord. Most of these revelations are condensed, and I would encourage readers to inquire of the Lord for deeper wisdom and understanding on these matters.

The collection is dedicated to my children. To keep that generation engaged, one must be concise, driving the sword of the Spirit with quick words while praying that you have their attention. Each "nugget" can be digested within minutes and pondered over for hours, provoking thought and inciting questions.

My prayer is that all ages would read these "nuggets" and not walk away contented for having read them, but linger with each one, inviting the Holy Spirit to plant them as seeds in their spirits, that those seeds might grow and produce fruit in their lives.

With love,
Veronica Guard Weekes

Contents

NUGGET ONE

...On Entitlement

It is not a bad word, as interpreted by our contemporary vernacular, but a word that believers in Jesus Christ must embrace! We are entitled to everything Jesus Christ died for and all of the promises declared by the Most High God, who sent Jesus to prove the true character of His fatherhood.

Deuteronomy 33 lists the blessing Moses reiterated to the children of Israel before his departure and the handing over of his leadership to Joshua. Reiterated, because in Genesis 49 these very blessings were declared by Jacob to his sons before his death. The nation of Israel has its foundation in the sons of Jacob, each son representing a tribe of Israel—but in a few hundred years, oppressed by hard times and amid phenomenal events, the chosen of God forgot their entitlement and had to be reminded.

In this generation, we believers in Jesus Christ have been grafted onto the nation of Israel, and we are entitled to the very same blessings! Do not let the oppressive circumstances of this world keep you so overwhelmed with worry that you forget. The era from Moses to Jesus is considered the age of the "Law," but

Jesus did not dispense with the "Law." He said He came to fulfill the "Law." There are blessings within the "Law," and 2 Corinthians 1:20 declares that the blessings of the Lord are "Yea and Amen"—meaning "Yes and Let it Be." Embrace your *entitlement* to *all* of the blessings of old and new today.

A Place to Ponder on Entitlement

Consider Deuteronomy 33 and Genesis 49, and list the many blessings declared in these verses.

Challenge: Highlight the blessings that have not shown up in your life. Ponder on each one and pray to the Father in Jesus' name for its manifestation. You are entitled.

NUGGET TWO

...On Faith

We ask for more faith. We ask to strengthen our faith. We seem to doubt that our God has given us the capacity for faith (period) through our Lord Christ Jesus.

In the story from Mark 9:17-24, the man who brought his son to Jesus to be healed was disappointed that the disciples could not handle the one thing he desired. Healing and deliverance for his son irritated his heart. Parents will understand the niggling concern in every waking hour for a suffering child. The man cried for Jesus to have compassion "on us" (him and his son). Jesus first made it clear that all things are possible to them that believe. Just in case the man thought his faith might fail, he cried, "I believe; help THOU my unbelief" (Mark 9:24 KJV).

Smart man! He is saying here to Jesus, "YOU help my unbelief...my faith." We look to Jesus, the author and the finisher of our faith (Hebrews 12:2). He will provide the measure of faith we need to conquer every situation, as the situation arises.

A Place to Ponder on Faith

If you trust in Jesus and His finished work on the cross, you have all the faith you will ever need.

Challenge: Are there events or situations in your life that you think are hopeless? Call them out one at a time, so the Holy Spirit—our Helper sent by Jesus—hears your cry. "*Help*, Lord, and help my unbelief."

NUGGET THREE

...On Prayer

Children know how to get what they want from a parent. They know how to get a parent's full attention, which will inevitably yield the result they want. Keep in mind that the request is not always a need; the wants get answered too.

My children and grandchild have demonstrated this ability and have succeeded every time, and it has taken me decades to recognize the strategy. Have you ever observed a child holding a parent's face between their tiny hands, locking eyes, waiting for engagement and the parent's full attention, then sweetly launching their request? Whether it is for a bathroom break (need), or playing a game (fun), or going out for ice cream (want), the parent does not resist, and the child waits patiently for fulfillment of their request. When was the last time, beloved, that you were in Daddy God's face, making a request? He loves the intimacy, and He *will* answer (Isaiah 65:24; 1 John 5:14-15).

A Place to Ponder on Prayer

Know with confidence that our Daddy God hears us when we pray. Even the smallest whisper does not go unnoticed by Him.

Challenge: Revisit things you have prayed for or matters that concern you. Be in His face, and engage with a loving Father, and see Him answer you.

NUGGET FOUR

...On Damage Control

In business, the goal is to operate at an optimal level where all operations are in sync, producing the ideal product. It is the same in the home. A missing lightbulb in the kitchen or a faucet not working in the bathroom make the whole function of the home off-balance, requiring repairs. Today, there are business tactics to address discrepancies that hinder optimum production in the flow of business. The smart home uses technology to detect flaws and maintenance needs that prevent optimal performance. Life is in a perpetual state of damage control. Our Most High God has been dealing with damage control since the malfunction of the ultimate enterprise—the Garden of Eden. Throughout the Old Testament, God directed men to address flaws in His system (Judges 2:16) in a continuing quest for damage control. And then—more efficient than business tactics, more efficient than smart home technology—*Jesus* was sent by Father God to ultimately address every possible malfunction we can ever have in life. *Tetelestai*: It is finished (John 19:30)!

A Place to Ponder on Damage Control

It is finished! John 19:30 declares the finished redemptive process executed by our Lord Jesus Christ. Redemption comes with: salvation, divine health, financial blessing, peace, successful relationships, forgiveness, an escape route in any bad situation. But wait...there is more!

Challenge: Read the Book of Ruth in the Bible and identify the true redeemer. Note how Ruth and Naomi's life would have changed following the redemptive act at the gate.

...On Justification

The entire content of Romans 4, and continuing into Romans 5, is to help us understand that we are considered righteous because of our faith in the finished work of Jesus Christ. Faith is believing. Believing that in one quick action, God Himself, in the person of Jesus, came down from heaven and died on the cross; His blood was presented to the Father; He went to hell to disable the enemy of our lives and was resurrected from the dead as proof that He *did* what He was sent to do. Believing in the action of Jesus as the highest spiritual function that makes us righteous before God our Father. A simple, one-touch function on our computers corrects any misalignment on the document we are painstakingly preparing. One touch—justification—will adjust margins and realign the document to visual perfection. This is what Jesus did. One event, and we are visually perfect in our Father's eyes. We are justified!

A Place to Ponder of Justification

Once we are born again, having surrendered our lives to Jesus, when our Father looks at us, He sees a perfect person (Romans 4:7-8). We may not "feel" perfect, but in the spirit realm, where the real action is, we are perfect.

Challenge: Knowing this truth, can you think of at least two areas in your life that could be different (Romans 5:3-5; Romans 5:9)?

NUGGET SIX

...On Osmosis

"The movement of particles from an area of *high* concentration to an area of *low* concentration across a semi-permeable membrane" defines *osmosis*. The occurrence equalizes the concentration of materials on either side of the membrane. It is a smooth, subtle, or gradual absorption or mingling (dictionary. com). The Holy Ghost acts as that semi-permeable membrane, mingling our DNA with the DNA of our Most High God. The gradual process makes us more and more like Him. Not that we are not already, but we live in the realm of time, and we need the hours, days, months, and years of life's experiences to gradually become grounded (never moving, according to John 15:7) and growing into the new creature He is perfecting to wield His power. Patience with ourselves and forgiveness of others, who are also enduring the metamorphosis, are key ingredients for this joyous transition.

A Place to Ponder on Osmosis

I sense the process of osmosis in my own life. Maybe some areas have moved towards the *high* concentration sooner than others.

Challenge: Starting with three areas—patience, love, and forgiveness—consider your level of concentration and consciously request the help of the Holy Spirit to accelerate the process.

NUGGET SEVEN

...On Adoption

In our natural world, the stigma attached to adoption has caused hurt and a sense of rejection, because that is what the enemy of our souls has orchestrated. The purpose is to desensitize us to the original intent of our Father God, to the full acceptance enshrined in His adoption plan for us (Galatians 4:5-7). God wanted us and intentionally selected us, embracing us close to His heart, saying: "I love you; you are mine, and I will do whatever it takes to keep you near to Me." Full acceptance means that He wants us—with all our flaws and insecurities, with all our fears and iniquities. In the spirit world, adoption into the family of God is a privilege, and not a reason to carry a sense of rejection in our lives.

A Place to Ponder on Adoption

You might write a comment on social media, and no one acknowledges with a response, so you feel outside the clique, not belonging. No one laughed at your joke at the family dinner table, and you want to hide for the rest of the evening. With God, we are never shunned, always belonging, and known by all of heaven as His favorite.

Challenge: Be still in the Lord's presence and wait until the flood of His love hits you. Don't move until you hear "I love you," and "I will never leave you nor forsake you" (Deuteronomy 31:6; Psalm 55:22; Matthew 28:20).

NUGGET EIGHT

...On Women

"A woman is right by instinct, not by fact" (TD Jakes, 2021). This statement came from a man who had a revelation of the Lord God. If there is a boast in this statement, it is a boast of my God. Women do not need all the facts to reach a conclusion; they are wired to instinctively sense the truth about a situation—no facts, no references, just knowing with conviction what is the truth. The woman from Shunem In 2 Kings 4:8-9 "perceived" that Elisha was a man of God, and her hospitality toward him proved fruitful. Also, in 2 Kings 5:1-3, a young maid trusted in Elisha's ability as a prophet of God to heal Naaman, the captain of the host of the King of Syria. The woman, Rahab, in Joshua 2:12-21 saved her family with a red cord hanging from her window, because she instinctively recognized that there was something wonderfully different about those called the children of the Most High God. The woman Jael, in Judges 4:18-21, used her wit to destroy Sisera, the one who had tormented the Jews for years. She drove a tent peg into his temple, and with that instinctive act subdued the oppressors of Israel so that the land had rest for forty years (Judges 5:31). In John 20:1-

18, Mary Magdalene reported that the Lord was not in the tomb and returned with two disciples who confirmed the fact. The men left to go to their homes, but Mary Magdalene doggedly and instinctively remained, because she wanted the truth. The answer she received is still beneficial to us today. HE IS RISEN!

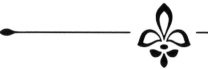

A Place to Ponder on Women

When was the last time you gave credit to a woman in your life (wife, mother, sister, aunt, cousin, even your neighbor or employee) who gave good, accurate counsel that added value to your life?

Challenge: Write a note expressing your gratitude to two women in your life who gave good counsel to you and benefitted your life.

NUGGET NINE

...On the First-Born

"First-born," "first-fruits," and "tithe" are all synonymous. Meaning, the terms carry the same power, reap the same benefits—and most importantly, they all belong to the Most High God. In 2 Kings 4:42-44, a man from Baalshalisha came to Elisha with his first-fruits: twenty loaves of barley bread and ears of corn. There were with Elisha the sons of the prophets, one hundred in number, still hungry after a little soup, and Elisha commanded his servant to give to the men. Just like in the New Testament (Matthew 14:14-21, Mark 6:30-44, Luke 9:10-17, John 6:5-14), when Jesus multiplied the food enough for the crowd to be filled and satisfied with leftovers. The same result with Elisha—there was enough to satisfy one hundred men with leftovers. Malachi 3:10 is clear that the tithe and offerings (first-fruits) presented to God generate power and anointing to get wealth. Romans 11:16 confirms that if the first-fruits are holy, the entire thing is holy. The same with the tithe. If the first ten percent is given back to God, the entire thing will produce more, being made holy by the tithe. The first-born, born through the matrix of his/her mother, transcending from the spirit world to the physical, belongs to God and carries the power and anointing to get wealth. Wealth of wisdom, wealth of authority, wealth in material abundance, and an overwhelming ability to overcome the enemy. Jesus, the first-born of the Father, demonstrated that power in all that He did. Will all of the first-born raise their hands and present themselves unto God as His divine property?

A Place to Ponder on the First-Born

You may or may not have raised your hand, but if you did, your challenge is clear.

Challenge: Everyone is obligated to give back to God what is His (Mark 12:17). Identify your first-fruits, determine your tithe, be deliberate in finding God-inspired activities, and give back to Him.

NUGGET TEN

...On Grafting

In the Apostle Paul's letter to the Roman church (Romans 11:17-18 ESV), he writes: "But if some of the branches were broken off, and you, although a wild olive shoot, were grafted in among the others and now share in the nourishing root of the olive tree, do not be arrogant toward the branches." Much substance is in these verses, but the focus for us, the Gentiles, is sharing in the "nourishing root of the olive tree."

One feature of grafted trees is that grafted trees reproduce the fruit, characteristics, and structure of the plant in which it is propagated. Branches grafted onto trees with certain rootstock will grow faster and develop quicker than if left on their own. Grafting a plant whose roots are prone to a soil disease onto a rootstock that is resistant to that disease would allow that plant to grow successfully where it would otherwise have problems. The scientists also say that a disadvantage of grafting is that new varieties cannot be developed.

Disadvantage, scientists say—but for the believer in Jesus Christ, this is the best news and the biggest advantage of being grafted onto the divine olive tree of God. Our variety only comes from remaining in *Him*. John 15:5 promises the fruit, John 15:7 promises the characteristic, and John 15:16 promises the structure. The "rootstock" referred to for the believer is the Lord Jesus Christ. The condition is that we abide in His Word, we abide in His love, and we love one another. We acknowledge our "new variety" status from Deuteronomy 14:2 (and reiterated in 1 Peter 2:9). We are content to be a peculiar people unto our Lord. Let us go forth to conquer!

A Place to Ponder on Grafting

Being a conqueror and overcoming the enemy of our soul only comes from being rooted in Christ from our grafted-in position.

Challenge: In John 15, the fruit, characteristic, and structure are evidence of successful grafting. Can you name a specific fruit, characteristic, or structure already reflected in your life? Let's search for areas where we can improve.

Notes

Notes

Notes

Epilogue

With the "nuggets" digested, what happens next? The blessings emerging from the writings are intended for every reader, because our compassionate God desires for *all* to be saved, believe in Jesus Christ, and come to the knowledge of the truth (1 Timothy 2:4). If you have not made that commitment yet, please say and sincerely mean the prayer below:

Lord Jesus, I believe that You are the Son of the Most High God, who came from heaven to die, defeat the enemy of my soul, and resurrect in victory just for me. I renounce the devil and his influence in my life, and I declare that I am born again, justified by the blood of Jesus, and ready to live just for You, Lord. I call for Your help, Holy Spirit, in Jesus' name I pray. Amen.

About the Author

Veronica Guard Weekes was born and grew up in Castries, St. Lucia. After getting baptized in 1995, she committed herself to what matters to God, despite ridicule from friends and family. Her biggest desire is to see others come to Christ and experience that unexplainable peace that remains, even in the darkest hour. She married in 2000 and moved to Atlanta, Georgia, where she lives with her husband and children. A teacher by vocation, her calling is to teach the concerns of the Lord as He has taught her.

She holds a bachelor's degree in public administration from the University of the West Indies (Cave Hill, Barbados) and a master's degree in business administration with a major in hospitality from Keller Graduate School of Management (Atlanta, Georgia). She considers herself a lifelong learner and truly believes that God prospers us "even as our souls prosper" (3 John 1:2 KJV).